Bats are the only mammals that can really fly,
and flight has made them very successful.
There are more than nine hundred species, living in
almost every habitat from subarctic tundra to
tropical forests and deserts. Birds may rule the air
by day, but bats are the monarchs of the night.

This book is about one of the pipistrelle bats.
Pipistrelles are found around the world,
from North America to Africa, Europe,
Asia and Australia.

For Henry Venner Woodcock and his big brothers,
Alfie and Thomas
N.D.

For Ailsa
S.F-D.

First published 2001 by Walker Books Ltd
87 Vauxhall Walk, London SE11 5HJ

This edition published 2008

4 6 8 10 9 7 5 3

Text © 2001 Nicola Davies
Illustrations © 2001 Sarah Fox-Davies

The right of Nicola Davies and Sarah Fox-Davies to be identified as author and illustrator
respectively of this work has been asserted by them in accordance with the Copyright,
Designs and Patents Act 1988

This book has been typeset in Cochin and Sanvito

Printed in China

British Library Cataloguing in Publication Data:
a catalogue record for this book is available from the British Library

ISBN 978-1-4063-1275-1

www.walker.co.uk

BAT LOVES THE NIGHT

Nicola Davies

illustrated by

Sarah Fox-Davies

WALKER BOOKS
AND SUBSIDIARIES
LONDON · BOSTON · SYDNEY · AUCKLAND

Bat is waking,
upside down as usual,
hanging by her toenails.

Her beady eyes open.
Her pixie ears twitch.

She shakes her
thistledown fur.

She unfurls her wings,
made of skin so fine the finger bones
inside show through.

This pipistrelle bat
is no bigger than
your thumb.

A bat's wing is its
arm and hand.
Four extra-long fingers
support the skin of the wing.

Bats' toes are shaped like hooks,
so it's no effort for a bat to hang
upside down.

Now she unhooks her toes
and drops into black space.
With a sound like a tiny umbrella
opening, she flaps her wings.

Bat is flying.

Out!

Out under the broken tile
into the night-time garden.

Over bushes, under trees,
between fence posts,
through the tangled hedge
she swoops untouched.
Bat is at home in the darkness,
as a fish is in the water.
She doesn't need to see –
she can hear where she is going.

Bats can see. But in the dark, good ears
are more useful than eyes.

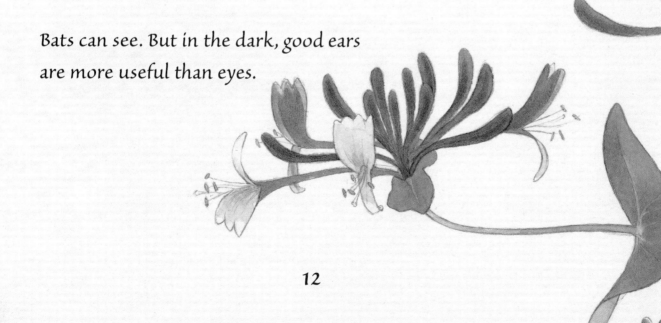

12

Bat shouts as she flies, louder than
a hammer blow, higher than a squeak.
She beams her voice around her like a
torch, and the echoes come singing back.
They carry a sound-picture of all
her voice has touched.
Listening hard, Bat can hear every
detail, the smallest twigs, the
shape of leaves.

*Using sound to find your way like this
is called echolocation.
Some bats shout through their mouth,
and some shout through their nose.*

Gliding and fluttering
back and forth,
she shouts her torch of
sound amongst the trees,
listening for her supper.

All is still...

15

Then a fat moth takes flight below her.

Bat plunges, fast as
blinking, and grabs it in
her open mouth.

But the moth's pearly
scales are moon-dust
slippery. It slithers from
between her teeth.

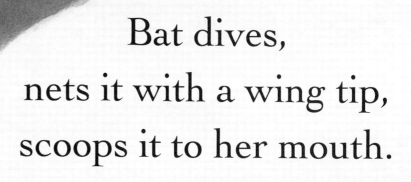

Bat dives,
nets it with a wing tip,
scoops it to her mouth.

This time she bites hard.
Its wings fall away, like the
wrapper from a toffee.
In a moment the moth is eaten.
Bat sneezes.
The dusty scales got up her nose.

18

Hunting time has run out.
The dark will soon be gone.
In the east the sky is getting light.
It's past Bat's bedtime.

The place where bats sleep in the day is called a roost.
It can be in a building, a cave, or a tree, so long as it's dry and safe.

She flies to the roof in the last shadows,
and swoops in under the broken tile.

21

Inside there are squeakings.
Fifty hungry batlings hang in a huddle,
hooked to a rafter by outsized feet.
Bat lands and pushes in amongst them,
toes first, upside down again.

Baby bats can't fly.
Sometimes mother bats carry their babies when
they go out, but mostly the babies stay behind in the roost
and crowd together to keep warm.

Bat knows her
baby's voice, and
calls to it.

The velvet scrap
batling climbs aboard
and clings to her fur
by its coat-hanger feet.

24

Wrapped in her
leather wings,
it suckles
Bat's milk.

Baby bats drink mother's milk until
they learn to fly at a few weeks old.
Then they can leave the roost
at night to find their own food.

Outside the birds are singing.
The flowers turn their faces to the sun.
But inside the roof hole,
the darkness stays.
Bat dozes with her batling,
waiting.

Bats are nocturnal. That means they rest by day
and come out at night to search for food.

27

When the tide of night rises again
Bat will wake, and plunge
into the blackness, shouting.

Bat loves the night.

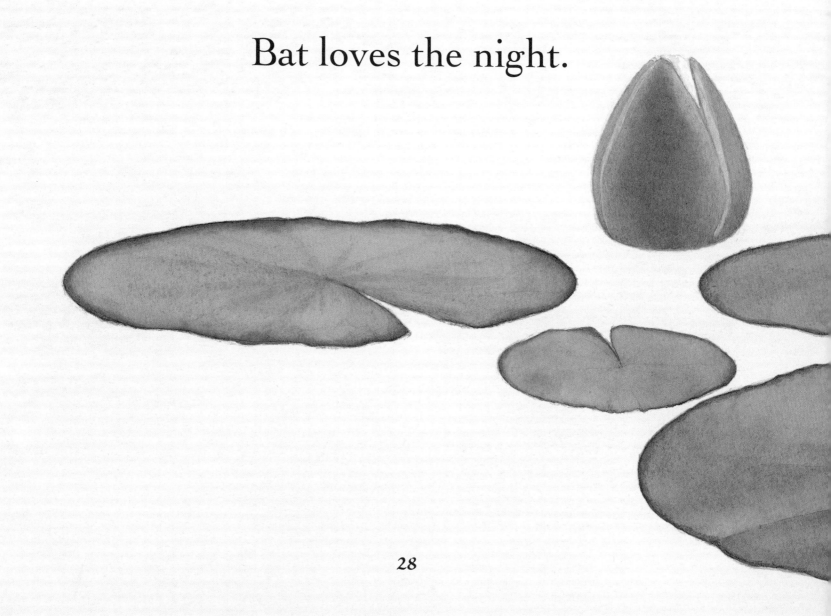

Index

Look up the pages to find
out about all these batty things.
Don't forget to look at both
kinds of word –
this kind and
this kind.

Mexican freetail bat
(Tadarida brasiliensis)

About the Author

Nicola Davies is a zoologist who has
studied all kinds of mammals, from whales
in the Indian Ocean and Newfoundland
to bats in west Wales. She is also the
acclaimed author of many books for
children, including the Nature Storybooks
Ice Bear, *One Tiny Turtle*, *Big Blue Whale* and
White Owl, Barn Owl. She lives in Devon.

About the Illustrator

Sarah Fox-Davies loves to draw wild
animals in their natural environments.
The many books she has illustrated for
children include the bestselling *Little Beaver
and the Echo* by Amy Macdonald and the
Nature Storybook, *Walk With a Wolf*
by Janni Howker – which was shortlisted
for the Kurt Maschler Award and
Highly Commended for the TES
Junior Information Book Award.
She lives in Wales.

Praise for Nature Storybooks...

"For the child who constantly asks How? Why?
and What For? this series is excellent."
The Sunday Express

"A boon to parents seeking non-fiction picture books to read
with their children. They have excellent texts
and a very high standard of illustration to go with them."
The Daily Telegraph

"As books to engage and delight children, they work superbly.
I would certainly want a set in any primary
classroom I was working in."
Times Educational Supplement

"Here are books that stand out from the crowd,
each one real and individual in its own right and
the whole lot as different from most other series non-fiction
as tasty Lancashire is from processed Cheddar."
Books for Keeps

Find notes for teachers about how to use Nature Storybooks in the classroom at
www.walker.co.uk/downloads

Nature Storybooks support KS 1-2 Science